LET THE HEALING BEGIN!

Workbook

GUIDED, PRACTICAL PATHWAYS TO HEALING
MOTHER-DAUGHTER RELATIONSHIPS

IMOGENE BROWN-ROBINSON

Contributions by Imojean Lois Robinson, L.L.M.S.W., Clinical and Family Therapist

ISBN 978-1732458222
Printed in the United States of America
First Printing, 2019

DISCLAIMER

*The information in this book is for general use, and not meant to replace the support, assistance and/or treatment of a medical professional and/or professional therapist or counselor. The authors and publisher advise readers to take full responsibility for their emotional health and well-being and know their limits. Some exercises involve revisiting experiences that may have caused challenging emotions and/or trauma, therefore **<u>PLEASE CONSULT WITH YOUR CLINICAL PROFESSIONAL before beginning this workbook if you are under psychiatric care or seeing a therapist for clinical depression or any other mental disorder.</u>***

It is recommended that anyone under 16 years of age be assisted by an adult in the use of this workbook.

Table of Contents

Preface

*Too often we make "positive confessions", or, as Christians we "confess" things from the Word of God without **cooperating** with that confession or that word. We confess, "I love you with the love of the Lord", without taking the steps to live that love out loud. We confess, "I can do all things through Christ, who strengthens me", while at the same time finding it too difficult to forgive.*

*The pathway to healing is trod by a series of **choices**. Some choices we will need to make daily - some may be a one-time deal, but we can rest assured that every time we choose to forgive, to love in spite of... to take the high road... God is there to help us execute that decision; in other words, whenever we say "YES" to His will (and it is ALWAYS His will for us to love and to forgive), **He empowers us to live out that choice.***

Can a person forgive if they are not a believer in Jesus? Certainly, they can, however, those who believe and have accepted Jesus as Lord and Savior are able to access the Holy Spirit, who reside in us and empowers us to forgive in any situation ..."just as God in Christ also has forgiven you."

I encourage you to keep these scriptures and quotes in mind as you go through this workbook, not merely to recite but to understand, to make them come alive in your everyday walk; to make them your own.

"I can do all things through Him who strengthens me.."   *Philippians 4:13 (NASB)*

"...walk in love, just as Christ also loved you and gave Himself up for us..."
                                                                        Ephesians 5:2 (NASB)

**"Be kind to one another, tender-hearted, forgiving each other, just as God
in Christ also has forgiven you."**
                                                                        Ephesians 4:32 (NASB)

**"Forgiveness is an act of the will, and the will can function regardless of the
temperature of the heart."**
                                                                        Corrie Ten Boom

"I CAN, if I WILL!"   *I. L. Brown-Robinson*

This book is for you. It will contain your private, intimate, transparent thoughts. It is going to be life-changing for you – not the book alone but coupled with your open-ness and your honesty, your life will never be the same. I recommend that you keep it in a safe place. Although you may be instructed or prompted to share certain entries, thoughts or resolutions, I strongly suggest you do not share this book with anyone <u>UNLESS you are inviting them to be a part of YOUR healing process.</u>

You will be instructed to write things concerning your mother and/or your daughter – personal, private things; <u>these things are not yours to share</u> - they are from YOUR prospective and you are asked to write them ONLY for the sake of HEALING – YOUR healing. To share them with anyone other than a counselor *(professional and/or spiritual),* and possibly a spouse, would be putting your healing process at risk.

Many times, a person going through the healing process, once they begin to be enlightened, will get a sense of hope and confidence. This is awesome, and I want that for you, however - with that can come the temptation to abort the process and "handle it on my own". Stopping the healing process prematurely can cause wounds to heal on the surface without healing on the inside. Issues can hide this way, becoming deeper and more toxic than before, making it very difficult – more uncomfortable to revisit these issues; as a result, the relationship continues to suffer and may never be completely healed; never come close to its maximum potential.

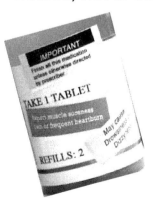 About three days after taking antibiotics, we feel so much better; the feeling of RELIEF suggests to our bodies that the threat is gone and no longer a need to take the medication. Usually there is a statement written on the prescription bottle as well as the patient information sheet: **"Finish all medication unless otherwise directed by your physician or prescriber",** some even add, **"even if you feel better".** The reason is that if treatment stops too soon, the drug may not kill **all** the bacteria. You may become sick again, and the remaining bacteria may become resistant to the antibiotic that you've taken.

The process of healing in a relationship is like peeling back an onion – there are many layers; the deeper the wounds, the more layers that need to be peeled. Therefore – celebrate every step as a milestone but STAY THE COURSE! Even when it seems repetitive, and it will, stay the course – finish it to the end.

Let the book and the workbook do what they are designed to do.

This book is loaded with thoughts, instructions and exercises that will stir up your emotions. PACE YOURSELF; take short breaks when needed, in order to reflect and go through the process.

I recommend no more than a chapter or 2 per day; taking in too much at a time will not allow you to gain the desired and necessary results – your emotions need time for full processing.

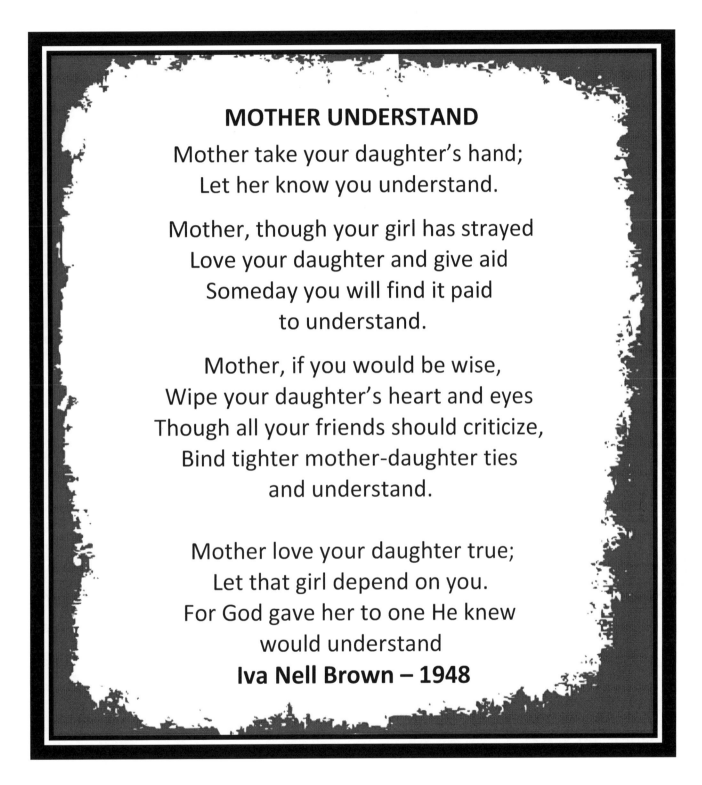

MOTHER UNDERSTAND

Mother take your daughter's hand;
Let her know you understand.

Mother, though your girl has strayed
Love your daughter and give aid
Someday you will find it paid
to understand.

Mother, if you would be wise,
Wipe your daughter's heart and eyes
Though all your friends should criticize,
Bind tighter mother-daughter ties
and understand.

Mother love your daughter true;
Let that girl depend on you.
For God gave her to one He knew
would understand
Iva Nell Brown – 1948

CHAPTER 1

The Conversation

"Wanting to obey the Lord, without dishonoring my mom, I asked God to lead me in the conversation – the timing, the words...I had no idea how to present this to my mom..."

From "Let the Healing Begin!" page 3, par. 3

In this chapter, I shared a conversation that normally would have been very difficult. Instead, because of these principles, it was the sweetest and most healing conversation I ever had with my mom. We need the leading and the insight of the Helper to guide us and to prepare our hearts to walk through difficult conversations, whether we are the initiator or the one who is confronted. Confrontation is not always a bad thing, but our goal should always be peace, healing and forgiveness. We need to make sure we enter the conversation with a changed heart, wanting to understand and be understood, rather than wanting to be right; wanting to win and the other person lose.

3 principles for starting and working thru difficult conversations...
(more in the appendix)

PRAY for WISDOM:
- *the right words to say*
- *the right timing*
- *sensitivity to the other person*
- *when to stop talking, or change the subject*

PREFACE your discussion:
- *State your purpose for initiating the conversation*
- *State your heart concerning the situation*
- *State your expectation for the outcome of the conversation*

PROTECT the GOOD in the relationship:
- *Be intentional; focus directly on the present issues*
- *Don't unnecessarily open wounds that are healing.*
- *Give grace – a way out; if they apologize, choose to forgive.*
- *Work on accepting where YOU are, and where THEY are.*
- *Pause if necessary, and come back to the conversation to closure*

I need to have a conversation with my MOTHER / DAUGHTER. *(circle one)*

Answering the following questions will help locate where you are, and help you decide whether you are truly ready to have the conversation.

What am I wanting to gain from this conversation?

_____
_____
_____
_____
_____
_____.

I expect that as a result of this conversation _____

_____

_____.

I will protect the relationship by _____

_____

_____.

NOTES...

_____
_____
_____
_____
_____
_____
_____
_____
_____
_____

"I remember explicitly as a child, having the very strong inclination to identify with my mom – that I was to be like her. Again, I never thought about it – it was just "in me" to be like her. We sometimes underestimate the power of influence over our children..."

"Let the Healing Begin!" page 14, par. 1

"...With your words, you can put your daughter in a box from which she may never escape – you, as one of her greatest protectors and influencers, may very well be putting your daughter in bondage with your words." **"Let the Healing Begin!" page 19, par. 1**

Influence: the capacity to have an effect on the character, development, or behavior of someone or something, or the effect itself.

"You will influence, POSITIVELY or NEGATIVELY"
We don't think about this often, but every decision we make and everything we do is influenced by someone or something - whether it's something we read, something we were taught or saw someone do; what we believe and even our opinions are framed by the things that have influenced us – good or bad. Mom, your daughter is watching you, and she's going to do what you DO – not just what you say to do.

Observational / Experiential Learning

We are constantly learning as human beings, whether intentionally or subconsciously. Children are especially vulnerable; they learn more by what they observe and what they experience than by what you tell them. Be intentional about what you want your child to learn from you.

Think about what or who has influenced you and how you are influencing those around you. In this lesson, we particularly want to look at the generational influences *(also referred to as intergenerational influences)* that have created dysfunctional practices in your family, that have been and continue to be passed down to the next generation. The objective is to identify dysfunction, or what is NOT working, and replace it with healthy, functional practices.

1. Name 3 ways you have been influenced by your mother.
(this may include Grandma, adoptive, surrogate, or whoever was "mother" to you)

Positive

1. _____

2. _____

3. _____

Negative

1. _____

2. _____

3. _____

2. Name 3 ways that you influence your daughter, if applicable.
(may include niece, granddaughter, surrogate/foster, etc.)

Positive

1. _____

2. _____

3. _____

Negative

1. _____

2. _____

3. _____

If applicable, how is your daughter's influence with her daughter?
Fantastic_____   Great_____   Good_____   OK_____   Needs Help_____

*I see a pattern of **positive** influence. I need to continue* _____

_____

_____

_____

_____

_____

_____

_____ .

*I see a pattern of **negative** influence. I need to change* _____

_____

_____

_____

_____

_____

_____ .

Which is YOUR daughter's greater influence; you, or social media?

Social media does not regard our families when deciding to distribute negative and inappropriate blogs, shows, videos – media! Is her self-esteem at the mercy of Facebook "likes" or "loves"? Does she look to her Facebook "friends" for advice, acceptance and affirmation? If applicable, are there guidelines and boundaries set for her on social media?

_____

_____

_____

_____

_____

CHAPTER 3
The "Mother Love" or "Mother Wound"

"We are biologically programmed to look to our mothers for nurturing. And as our mothers did, we also tend to learn nurturing from the generational line of women before us; if they developed healthy mother-daughter bonds, our chances for like relationships are great. However, when that emotional need is not met, it upsets a fundamental balance throughout our childhood that, without divine intervention, can plague us for the rest of our lives."
                                                    "Let the Healing Begin!" page 28, par. 1

In this chapter, we discussed:
- Some nurturing characteristics of a mother's love
- How we learn nurturing, or the lack of nurturing, which can cause generational dysfunction
- How a daughter is affected if she does not receive the "mother's love"
- The "mother wound" that can develop due to a lack of "mother's love"

Nurturing *(nurture):* Help develop; to take care of, feed, and protect someone or something, especially young children or plants, and help him, her, or it to develop.

Again, the goal here is not to blame our mothers and grandmothers, but rather to identify the dysfunction AND to see what healthy practices we can build on. Mind you, we're not focusing on **people**, but rather the **behaviors and though processes** that have been prevalent in our families. We're not labeling **people** as dysfunctional, but rather identifying the habits, the strongholds and the mindsets that caused hardship and heartache in our families – the things that did not work well for us. It is equally important to see the good – to identify, appreciate and capitalize on any good, healthy, functional tendencies.

Were there any family traditions that worked well? Let's hold fast to those; rekindle them if they were discontinued – these are the things that bring unity; the glue that holds the family together.

Attachment Theory: Importance of Bonding with Child

Your daughter needs a secure attachment for healthy development in the following domains: social, emotional, mental, and psychological. The bond that you create starting at infantry, will impact their future outcome in these areas. It is important to establish a bond to avoid "mother wounds". Studies have indicated that the bond, or wound, created from the caretaker *(in this instance, we are using mothers)* is a huge predictor of how well your child will advance or develop.

Secure Attachment

Secure Attachment is not simply the care you provide for a child, or verbally communicating love to your child; a secure attachment is primarily based on the quality of **nonverbal communication** between you and your child *(mostly established during infancy)*. Types of secure attachment development are:

- looking in the eyes with care
- rubbing them on their head
- cheek to cheek
- hugging
- other physical forms of love

Physical forms of love also help stimulate the brain in both infants, and children even into young adult age. Developing these non-verbal forms of communication will help to deepen the relationship between you and our child/ren. A child is more reluctant to confide in, communicate with a parent who they feel is unsafe and/or lacks the capacity to handle their *(the child's)* emotional, mental, social, hormonal or psychological battles/frustrations/needs.

Children who feel emotionally disconnected from their primary caregiver are likely to feel confused, misunderstood, and insecure, no matter how much they are loved.

Some issues that impact the Secure Attachment Bond

– Daily stressors, inhibiting your ability to concentrate on the needs of your child, and therefore, neglecting your child's needs/discounting them.

– Emotional/Mental stressors that impede your ability to focus on your child. Issues such as depression, anxiety, grieving, or just being overly occupied can affect your child's ability to rely on you as a "safe place"/trusted place for them to confide in. As a result, it causes a breakdown in the attachment.

– Infants who are sickly, or cry excessively, causing burnout in the parent.

An infant could also affect his/her own emotional well-being if he/she has emotional, psychological, or mental deficits that interfere with the caregiver making non-verbal connections.

Older Children and Secure attachment

When a child does not feel that the care giver cares for and understands them, the world can feel like an unsafe place, causing them to lose trust in themselves and others. This type of lack of secure attachment may result in the older child acting out displaying problematic behaviors, so as to get attention.

Attachment can be disrupted if the care giver is not consistent with how they provide for the child; sometimes they care for them, other times they don't represent inconsistency.

Child maltreatment is a huge disruption in the secure attachment bond.

Developing Secure attachment through non-verbal cues

Non-verbal cues are signals that are communicated through tone of voice, touch, or facial expression.

Eye Contact: Look at your child affectionately *(even through adulthood)*, this will help the child feel relaxed, safe, and happy; a core part of helping to establish self esteem & understanding.

Facial Expression: Your child picks up on your emotions. If you are projecting fear, sadness, depression, anger and negative emotions for most of the time, your child will experience feelings of unsafe, unsure, uncertainty, and ultimately take on feelings of stress as well.

Tone: Children pick up on different tones: harsh, indifferent, preoccupied, tenderness, interest... are all tones that a child takes in. Be mindful of the tones that are being demonstrated to your child. Tone is very important in communication; by communicating and using tone strategically, your child will gain a sense of trust and confidence.

When using tone for older children, it is important that your demand, request, or whatever is communicated, matches the tone of what is wanting to be conveyed, or it will lead to unsurety.

Touch: A child can pick up on your emotional state, through your touch. Hugging, nurturing, etc. helps a child to relax more.

Imojean Lois Robinson, L.L.M.S.W.

Sometimes, planned or unplanned, we find ourselves raising children with no specific idea as to what it should look like – we don't necessarily examine our expectations.

By answering the following question, you will:

1. *Paint a clear picture of what good mothering looks like and set a standard for yourself.*

2. *Begin to see clearly some of the expectations and/or biases you may have placed on your own mother.*

What does the ideal mother look like to you?
List some of her characteristics.

_____

_____

_____

_____

The first part of this exercise asks you to look for patterns in the practices of your mother, your maternal grandmother and yourself. Once we see the patterns, we want to accentuate the positive and eliminate the negative.

1.   My grandmother *(mom's mother)* **was _____ toward my mom.**
(circle all that apply)

loving   nurturing   affectionate   said "I love you"   helpful
supportive   encouraging   attentive   gentle   understanding
said kind words   protective   generous   hugged often
considerate   polite   thoughtful   selfless   forgiving
(other) _____   _____   _____   _____

mean   verbally abusive   physically abusive   sexually abusive
harsh   quarrelsome   selfish   uncaring   inconsiderate
accusing   conniving   unaffectionate   disparaging   dishonest
unforgiving   emotionally absent   unforgiving
(other) _____   _____   _____   _____

2. **My MOTHER is/was (*circle all that apply*) toward me.**

loving   nurturing   affectionate   said "I love you" helpful
supportive   encouraging   attentive   gentle   understanding
said kind words   protective   generous   hugged often
considerate   polite   thoughtful   selfless   forgiving
(other) _____   _____   _____   _____

mean   verbally abusive   physically abusive   sexually abusive
harsh   quarrelsome   selfish   uncaring   inconsiderate
accusing   conniving   unaffectionate   disparaging   dishonest
unforgiving   emotionally absent   unforgiving
(other) _____   _____   _____   _____

3. **I am (*circle all that apply*) to my daughter.**

loving   nurturing   affectionate   say "I love you" helpful
supportive   encouraging   attentive   gentle   understanding
say kind words   protective   generous   hug often
considerate   polite   thoughtful   selfless   forgiving
(other) _____   _____   _____   _____

mean   verbally abusive   physically abusive   sexually abusive
harsh   quarrelsome   selfish   uncaring   inconsiderate
accusing   conniving   unaffectionate   disparaging   dishonest
unforgiving   emotionally absent   unforgiving
(other) _____   _____   _____   _____

1. **What repeated words did you circle in numbers 1 and 2?**

_____

_____

_____

2. **What repeated words did you circle in numbers 2 and 3?**

_____

_____

_____

*I see a pattern of **positive** nurturing. I **need to** continue....*

_____

_____

So, I CHOOSE to _____

_____.

*I see a pattern of **negative** nurturing. I **need to** change....*

_____

_____

So, I CHOOSE to _____

_____.

*Remember that THINKING ABOUT changing, RECOGNIZING that you NEED TO change, and even WANTING TO change; NONE of these bring about a change. You must **CHOOSE** to change, **DETERMINE** what you will do to make those changes, and then **FOLLOW THROUGH**.*

*(This may be a good time to grab a "prayer partner" – someone you trust to keep your confidence....) **"...confess your sins to one another and pray for one another so that you may be healed."** James 5:16*

"We're all in this together!"
First Lady Kathy Lancaster

CHAPTER 4
You Can't Give What You Don't Have

"Tragically, for some reason, she had it in her mind that when you hold a baby it spoil them, so... we were not allowed; not even to feed him his bottle....With nothing to compar this to, not having seen how anyone else does it, and after all, I'm eight and she is m mother, I concluded that this is the way to raise a child; the proper way, of course, becaus this is Mommy, and Mommy is right."

"Let the Healing Begin!" page 31, par.

"To this day, I cannot recall ever hearing her mom tell her "I love you", nor have I ever heard her say it to her mom. And she could not impart to us what she did not have, nor teach us what she did not know." ***"Let the Healing Begin!" page 31, par. 3***

Think about it for a moment – what if **unconditional love** is something you mom has never experienced? What if the only form of discipline she received was quietly kept abuse...and that's all she knew...so that's all she could give?

In this chapter, we focused on one of the most common reasons that mothers fail to nurture their children – they just simply don't know how. It's not a good feeling for a young mother to discover that she doesn't really know how to nurture her child. But let's face it – sometimes you don't know, and you don't know that you don't know.

---

stronghold: a place that has been fortified so as to protect it against attack: fortress
a place where a particular cause or belief is strongly defended or upheld:

Strongholds, for this discussion, are those strong negative beliefs and emotions hurtful, damaging, and toxic behaviors and patterns that have been perpetuated through generations.

In this exercise, we have 3 objectives:

1. Determine whether the "mother love" has been present, or the "mother wound" has been a stronghold in your family *(specifically between you and your mom/daughter).*

2. Begin to forgive and show compassion to your mom who may not have been equipped to nurture you.

3. Become teachable in order that you can learn how to love and nurture your daughter(s).

1. What are some good examples of "Mother love", or nurturing that you experienced growing up?

_____

_____

_____

_____

_____

_____

2. Which of those examples have you applied (*or will you apply*) in raising your daughter(s)?

_____

_____

_____

_____

3. What are some examples of poor nurturing, neglect or abuse that you experienced growing up?

_____

_____

_____

_____

4. Which of those examples have you applied in raising your daughter(s)?

_____

_____

_____

_____

Is there a pattern?

I have seen my grandmother and/or my mother do this...(write the pattern)

_____
_____
_____
_____
_____ .

As a result, I have done this....(write your patterns concerning your daughter(s)

_____
_____
_____
_____
_____
_____
_____
_____ .

Teachable: capable of being taught.: apt and willing to learn; favorable to teaching.

> **"The way of a fool is right in his own eyes,**
> **But a wise man is he who listens to counsel."**
> **Proverbs 12:15 NASB**

Rephrase this proverb in your own words.

_____
_____
_____
_____

Are you *teachable*?

1a. Who, if anyone, has been a positive influence in teaching you how to raise and love your daughter(s)?

_____

_____

1b. How were they helpful?

_____

_____

_____

_____

2. Why do you think you were able to take their advice?

_____

_____

_____

_____

3. Who, if anyone, has tried to teach or advise you and you could not, or would not, receive their advice?

_____

_____

4. What do you think was the reason it was difficult to receive their advice?

_____

_____

_____

_____

5. Looking back, are there ways you could have benefitted from their advice?

_____

_____

_____

Chapter 5
It's A Process
(The Process Begins With You)

"Shaken, chastised; remembering the lesson I'd 'learned' only days ago, I went to th[e] closet. As I leaned down to pick up LaVonne, who had by now stopped crying and just la[y] there on the floor, I felt so horrible, realizing that I had mistreated -- yes, abused -- m[y] precious young daughter...."   **"Let the Healing Begin!" page 38, par. 1**

"If you're beginning to see yourself, where to make some adjustments – don't condem[n] yourself! The fact that you are reading this book, and you continue reading, shows you[r] heart; that you want to do better."   **"Let the Healing Begin!" page 39, par. 3**

Process: *a series of actions or steps taken in order to achieve a particular end.*

The challenge of change is that *sometimes you have a change of heart before you have a change of mind*. Don't be discouraged with yourself if you find that after doing the same thing in the same way for 20, 30 or 50 plus years you are not able to turn it around in a couple weeks. You've watched the videos, read the book, maybe even listened to the audio...you've read the scriptures, you've fasted and prayed; you've rededicated your life to Christ[,] you've consecrated – you've even taken discipleship classes...*DON'T B[E] DISCOURAGED – be patient with yourself and with your daughter or you[r] mom - it's a PROCESS!*

A wound that heals properly heals on the **inside** as well as the **outside**. If i[t] heals on the outside but never heals on the inside, it can become septic[,] infection can set in, preventing the healing process and sometimes even causing death. Regardless of the pain, it must now be opened up, cleaned[,] and possibly drained in order to heal correctly. It takes endurance, patience and a resolve that you are going to cooperate with the doctor, no matter how painful, because you understand that it is a **process...** It has a specific beginning, a specific regimen and an expected end. As the patient, YOU decide whether or not to go through the process; *if you opt out you will continue to operate with dysfunction* – you can walk, perhaps even run, but with a limp, a crutch, a cane or even a wheelchair.

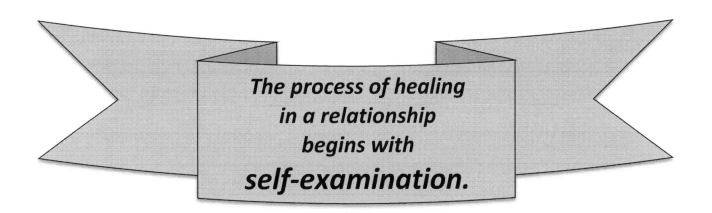

The process of healing in a relationship begins with **self-examination.**

To begin the process of healing and restoration, or mending in any relationship, you need to have a time of self-examination. This is the time to reflect, look at your OWN heart and make the necessary adjustments. You want to examine your attitudes and actions; also want to examine your motives – the intent of your heart. Before you address the conflicting issues with your mother or your daughter, you want to be sure that your goal and your purpose is mending the relationship and not just proving your side or winning.

Self-examination is not easy; it can be very uncomfortable, whether you are mom or daughter. If you are completely honest in the process, you will uncover and realize choices you've made and things you've done that you are not so proud of; things you wish you could take back - just as when I realized that I was abusive toward my daughter.

Forgiving yourself is a very necessary part of the process. I believe we all have regrets of one type or another, and it can be very difficult to get past regrets if we don't put it all in perspective. We've made some mistakes - some more than others, and some more detrimental than others, however, the biggest mistake of all would be to fall into the trap of self-condemnation. We need to keep moving forward, and in order to do that and see clearly, we need to rid ourselves of all the guilt and shame that seeks to keep us in mental and emotional bondage.

One Layer at a Time

These next 3 steps involve taking a very close, personal look at your life – pas and present, in order to reverse some of the negative effects of you experiences.

1. "To Go" List

For this exercise, you are going to write a list of the things that have **"to go!"** These are the things you have been holding against yourself; some are regret and some are grudges – everything you need to forgive yourself for. This i not a letter, it is a LIST – just like your grocery list, or your "to do" list. Be very specific. *(You may need to shred or burn the list after the exercise – and that' okay.)* Writing the list will help you to acknowledge and admit things you have tried to hide, even from yourself. Yes, it's going to be uncomfortable, but it's also going to be freeing; you're going to drop all the charges against yourself – you're going to take off the handcuffs.

When you forgive yourself, you are less apt to be defensive or lash out when confronted, and it becomes much easier to apologize and to forgive others. I you don't acknowledge and admit to yourself the things you are holding against yourself, they will continue to hide, to haunt and harass you and you will remain in the bondage of unforgiveness – toward yourself and toward others. God has forgiven you; others have forgiven you; it's time to let go o the guilt, the shame, the pain and the weight. HEALING BEGINS when you FORGIVE YOURSELF!

Now take the rest of the day to celebrate your freedom; do something nice for yourself! As you walk through these exercises, take the time to process and adjust to the new you – celebrate, let it marinate, take a deep breath – take a walk, smell some beautiful flowers- sing! That's what FREE people do!

2. The next step is to write a letter – to yourself.

This letter is for YOUR EYES ONLY, unless you decide to share it with someone. Be open, honest - say anything and everything you want to say to yourself. Don't rush through it. Don't write what you **think** you should say, write what you **want** to say. It's just you – being honest, completely honest with yourself. You have forgiven yourself, now write yourself a LOVE LETTER. If there's any residue of unforgiveness, go ahead and forgive yourself again. Ask yourself questions, give yourself answers – NO BOUNDARIES – say what's in your heart.

Your letter to yourself should be:
- **From you, TO YOU**

- **Hand-written**, *or whatever method you are comfortable with; the key is to be open, reflective, and honest with yourself.*

- **Focused toward at least one specific issue** you have been struggling with: the goal is....
  - to be open and honest with yourself
  - to let go of regrets and negative feelings toward yourself
  - to pour love on yourself – **unconditionally**

It doesn't matter if it's three pages or thirty; you will know when it's done.

Now take a break, and then read your letter, allowing healing to come as you read; take your time, don't rush through it. Respond to your letter in whatever way you need to, then move on to the next exercise.

3. This exercise involves re-visiting the experiences that have been life-altering to you. Because we are revisiting experiences that may have caused negative emotions, let me remind you to <u>PLEASE CHECK WITH YOUR CLINICAL PROFESSIONAL before beginning this exercise if you are under psychiatric care or seeing a therapist for clinical depression or any other mental disorder.</u>

Everyone has memories - some good, some bad; some are forgotten no sooner than they happen – if they have any effect, it's not long-lasting. And then there are those occurrences that have the potential to take us out of the game, or at best – alter our lives. These are the ones we are going after.

In this exercise, we are going back to those events, those incidents that crippled you – the ones you never got past, but you've been able to cover them with fake smiles. We're going after those incidents whose pain has been hiding behind illicit relationships, drugs and alcohol, "wilding-out" depression, hiding behind a "superior" attitude that hides the low self worth... no need to go on, you get it.

We've all heard and agree *(to some extent)* that you can't change the past. You are going to do just that! You are going to go back and UNDO some of the things that have been done to you. How on earth can I do that??? Glad you asked!

First, you must realize that whatever your experiences, good or bad, the lasting effect is not as much in your body *(if it was physical)* or to your property – even if it was destroyed, as it was in your MIND. Everybody has a story; why is it that two people can have the same identical story, same background and scenario but one survives and the other hits rock-bottom? Answer: because it is not the event or the incident(s) that change our lives, but the effect it has on our minds – the way we allow it to determine our future; the way we give it the power to change our story.

You are about to take your story back!

Take Back Your Story! *(The one God designed for you)*

For this exercise, you need to have the right atmosphere:

- You must be ALONE
- In a QUIET place
- Writing pad and pen/pencil
- TIME – as much time as you can spend,
  (I recommend at least 1-2 hours at a time)

In your QUIET place, with your pen and pad....

Divide your pages into AGE GROUPS: 1-3+, 4-6+, 7-10+, 11-14+, etc. The age groups are just to help you recall; you can broaden, narrow or even eliminate them. It doesn't matter if you don't recall the age, just try to recall the incidents.

Start with the first age group; go back as far as you can remember. Try to remember any incidents, good or bad, that you feel were life-changing. It doesn't have to be anything big – it can be as simple as "you had to go to bed and everyone else got to stay up late". If you believe it was life-altering - that it changed something in your story, let's revisit it. *(The purpose of bringing up the good ones is to retrieve and reinforce any positive effect it had on you.)* Take one incident at a time.

Ex. 1: I remember I was about 3... We were visiting relatives in Pennsylvania. Going into the house – it was dim; I had on a snowsuit – as my sister was taking it off, my mom said to put me to bed. I remember being carried through a hall and into a bedroom. No one else was in the room. She put me in a baby crib and left out of the room. I wasn't afraid, but I was very lonely. I cried and cried but no one came. After a while, my sister, Cassie, came into the room and gave me a bottle; I wanted her to take me out of the crib, but I knew she was not allowed. She left and I cried some more. A man came into the room – a very tall man, and very dark. There was a table in the room; he sat at the table and ate. I was glad to have someone in the room, even though he never said a word. He ate and left the room.

If I could have said anything to anyone, I would have said to my mom, "Please don't make me stay in this room alone." "Please let Cassie take me out of this crib – I feel abandoned!"

Although I can't go back and change this incident, in revisiting it I can allow myself to have a voice, which empowers me to eliminate the negative effec and to eliminate the feeling of being a victim. Remember, this is NOT abou making things happen differently; we can't do that, but what we CAN do i take control and change the effect it has on our MIND. No one can do this fo you but YOU.

Ex. 2: *I was 4 years old; my mom was in the hospital, older siblings at school. I was i afternoon kindergarten, but it was morning, so I was still at home. My dad was hom with me and my 2 younger sisters; one of them was a baby. I never saw them, but I knev they were there in the room with him. He came out of the bedroom, gave me fifteer cents and told me he needed me to go to the store, which was 2 blocks away, and ge some Pet-milk for my baby sister. I had never gone further than across the street to the schoolground by myself; but now -   I was a girl on a mission! I felt so grown up ano responsible. I went to the store, got the Pet-milk (the store-owner commented that I wa. very responsible), and came back home very quickly. My dad said he was proud of me. was very proud of myself; like there was nothing I couldn't do!*

In the first example, by revisiting, I was able to get my voice and change my story. In the second one, I was able to recapture the feeling of self-worth and reinforce that positive image - the spirit that God created ir me from birth. ***That's the real me!***

It doesn't matter how small or deep your situation is - let's go for all of it! Or the next page I will help you by giving you some specific questions to ask yourself in this process. Use the following pages to get you started; don't limit yourself to these pages, feel free to add your own notebook!

TAKE BACK YOUR ORIGINAL STORY!
(the one God designed for you)

1. **ATMOSPHERE:** Close your eyes. Try to remember everything you can about the incident – do everything you can to put yourself back in that place...remember the atmosphere; was it dark, light – what time of day or night was it? What did the place smell like? Was it wet, dry – hot, cold... try to remember everything. Write it down.

2. **WHO:** Keeping your eyes closed... Who was there? *(write it down)* Who SHOULD have been there? Who should NOT have been there? Who do you WISH was there?

3. **WHAT:** What happened? *(just facts, not how you FELT – that comes later).* Was it physical, verbal? Was it something you SAW or HEARD? Was it good or bad? What did they say to you? What were you saying to YOURSELF?

4. **HOW:** How did it make you feel? What was your take-away? In the first example, I felt abandoned; in the second, I felt empowered.

5. **CHANGE YOUR STORY:** If you could have said **anything** to **anybody,** what would you have said, and to whom? Write it down, as if you are there – say it to them. Say it until you are no longer a victim but empowered to move on!

    If it is a positive story, write your positive take-away;
    then repeat it until you believe it and retrieve it!

NOW SIT QUIETLY – just you and your Creator. If you need to forgive someone, *including yourself*, decide to do it now. Until you forgive, you are still a victim because the incident(s) still dictate and control your feelings. When you make the decision to forgive, God will help you every single time. Write down your thoughts; take a break, then move on to the next age group and go through the same process. *Freeing, isn't it?!*

TAKE BACK YOUR ORIGINAL STORY!

AGE at the time *(as close as you remember)* _____

1. **ATMOSPHERE:** *(describe your surroundings as much as you can)*

_____

_____

_____

2. **WHO:** *Who was there, not there, should have been, etc.*

_____

_____

_____

3. **WHAT:** *What happened?*

_____

_____

_____

_____

_____

_____

4. **HOW:** *How did it make you feel, or how did it affect you?*

_____

_____

_____

_____

5. **CHANGE YOUR STORY:** *What would you say, and to whom?*

_____

_____

_____

_____

_____

_____

TAKE BACK YOUR ORIGINAL STORY!

AGE at the time *(as close as you remember)* _____

1. **ATMOSPHERE:** *(describe your surroundings as much as you can)*

   _____
   _____
   _____

2. **WHO:** *Who was there, not there, should have been, etc.*

   _____
   _____
   _____

3. **WHAT:** *What happened?*

   _____
   _____
   _____
   _____
   _____

4. **HOW:** *How did it make you feel, or how did it affect you?*

   _____
   _____
   _____

5. **CHANGE YOUR STORY:** *What would you say, and to whom?*

   _____
   _____
   _____
   _____
   _____

TAKE BACK YOUR ORIGINAL STORY!

AGE at the time *(as close as you remember)* _____

1. **ATMOSPHERE:** *(describe your surroundings as much as you can)*

   _____

   _____

   _____

2. **WHO:** *Who was there, not there, should have been, etc.*

   _____

   _____

   _____

3. **WHAT:** *What happened?*

   _____

   _____

   _____

   _____

   _____

   _____

4. **HOW:** *How did it make you feel, or how did it affect you?*

   _____

   _____

   _____

   _____

5. **CHANGE YOUR STORY:** *What would you say, and to whom?*

   _____

   _____

   _____

   _____

   _____

TAKE BACK YOUR ORIGINAL STORY!

AGE at the time *(as close as you remember)* _____

1. **ATMOSPHERE:** *(describe your surroundings as much as you can)*

_____

_____

_____

2. **WHO:** *Who was there, not there, should have been, etc.*

_____

_____

_____

3. **WHAT:** *What happened?*

_____

_____

_____

_____

_____

_____

4. **HOW:** *How did it make you feel, or how did it affect you?*

_____

_____

_____

5. **CHANGE YOUR STORY:** *What would you say, and to whom?*

_____

_____

_____

_____

_____

TAKE BACK YOUR ORIGINAL STORY!

AGE at the time *(as close as you remember)* _____

1. **ATMOSPHERE:** *(describe your surroundings as much as you can)*

   _____

   _____

   _____

2. **WHO:** *Who was there, not there, should have been, etc.*

   _____

   _____

   _____

3. **WHAT:** *What happened?*

   _____

   _____

   _____

   _____

   _____

   _____

4. **HOW:** *How did it make you feel, or how did it affect you?*

   _____

   _____

   _____

   _____

CHANGE YOUR STORY: *What would you say, and to whom?*

_____

_____

_____

_____

_____

_____

"No doubt if, in the earlier years, Susanne's mom had not been addicted to alcohol, she would have been able to give her kids the proper nurturing and love. In a sense, she was a victim herself. It was not her own heart controlling her but the contents of the bottle, destroyer of lives and homes."   ***"Let the Healing Begin!" page 53, par. 2***

"My plea to you is to take a moment to see the bondage; that your mom was indeed a victim....why did she get drunk? What was hurting her? What was she trying to drown with the bottle?"   ***"Let the Healing Begin!" page 53, par. 3***

"What do you know about her life? About the things that damaged her self-esteem, crushed her dreams, set her back in her efforts to get ahead in life?"
                    "Let the Healing Begin!" page 67, par. 2

The objective of this group of chapters is to help you see past what you may see as your mom's failure to properly nurture, or love you with the "mother love", in light of the things she may have experienced that caused her, to whatever degree, to be a victim of her own circumstances - perhaps even her own decisions. We want to look at how these things affected her, how they may have affected you, and how we can prevent them from affecting your daughter.

In these chapters we address three things:

1. *Issues your mom may have carried into her adulthood.*
2. *Issues YOU may be carrying or have carried into YOUR adulthood.*
3. *Issues you may see in your daughter, that we can help her to resolve.*

This is not about giving or accepting excuses, but rather to get a clear, realistic picture of what has happened to your mom, and then to YOU as a result; what has happened to you, and then to YOUR DAUGHTER(S) as a result.

Part 1: About your MOTHER

Give a brief description, as far as you know, of **any** issues that your mother may have carried over from childhood, being mindful to recognize any patterns. **Select as many as apply.**

Ex. Hurt: *Deeply hurt by the way her parents treated her when she became pregnant.*

My mom may have carried these from her childhood...

Hurt _____

Anger _____

Abuse _____

Rejection _____

Low Self-esteem _____

Regret _____

Resentment _____

Incest _____

Rape _____

Molestation _____

Bullied _____

Bullying _____

Slow Learner _____

Learning Disability _____

ADD _____

Other _____

Now consider your mother's teenage and adult life...

My mom may have carried these from her teen and adult years...

Hurt _____

Anger _____

Abuse _____

Rejection _____

Low Self-esteem _____

Regret _____

Resentment _____

Incest _____

Rape _____

Molestation _____

Bullied _____

Bullying _____

Slow Learner _____

Learning Disability _____

ADD _____

Other _____

Addictions (alcohol) _____

Addictions (drugs) _____

Addictions (food) _____

Consider the WOMAN...

*Consider your mother now; **not as Mom, but as woman, before you were born.** Consider how thes issues may have impacted her life; not as excuses, but a reasons – as life-altering events over which she may hav had little or no control.*

Now that I have looked a little closer at my mom's earlier life, I am feeling/thinking...

_____

_____

_____

_____

_____

_____

_____

_____

_____

_____

_____

Although my mom is responsible for her own well-being, there may be some things I can do to help my mom make some positive steps;

_____

_____

_____

_____

_____

_____

_____

Part 2: About YOU

Give a brief description, as far as you know, of any issues that you may have carried over from your childhood. **Select as many as apply** and be as specific as you are comfortable with for each one. Remember this is for YOU – you don't have to share the information with anyone so be honest and open, that is key to your healing process and identifying negative patterns.

I have carried these from <u>my</u> childhood...

Hurt _____

Anger _____

Abuse _____

Rejection _____

Low Self-esteem _____

Regret _____

Resentment _____

Incest _____

Rape _____

Molestation _____

Bullied _____

Bullying _____

Slow Learner _____

Learning Disability _____

ADD _____

Other _____

Anger is often a secondary emotion. *Many times, a person's hurt, feeling of rejection, fear, grief, physical pain or other emotions are **expressed** as anger. This is true for children as well as adults, oftentimes without even realizing it. Whenever you see an expression of anger, whether in yourself or others, it is good to consider - what is at the root of this so often disguised emotion?*

*What are some of the things that might be expressed as anger in **your** life?*

_____

_____

_____

_____

_____

_____

_____

Do you recognize any other "hidden" or secondary emotions in your life?

_____

_____

_____

_____

_____

_____

Consider how these issues may have begun in your childhood, but not being resolved, carried over into your adulthood. In what ways do you think these things may have affected your daughter, or daughters if applicable? If you have more than one daughter, list them separately.

_____

_____

_____

_____

_____

Part 3: About YOUR DAUGHTER(S)

I believe that my daughter has had these issues from childhood...

Hurt _____

Anger _____

Abuse _____

Rejection _____

Low Self-esteem _____

Regret _____

Resentment _____

Incest _____

Rape _____

Molestation _____

Bullied _____

Bullying _____

Slow Learner _____

Learning Disability _____

ADD _____

Other _____

List 3 steps you can take to change the negative influences over your daughter(s).

1. _____

2. _____

3. _____

Recognizing the PATTERNS:

From the previous lists, describe the issues, if any, that are common among you and your mother.

_____

_____

_____

_____

_____

_____

_____

_____

_____

From the previous lists, describe the issues, if any, that are common among you and your daughter(s).

_____

_____

_____

_____

_____

_____

_____

_____

_____

_____

Once we have become aware of these issues, we are responsible to ourselves and to our daughters to make steps to heal dysfunctional relationships and practices. Take a moment to think about all you have learned; from reading the book, "Let the Healing Begin", from the book discussions, workshops, etc., from your prayer time and devotions listening to the Holy Spirit speaking to your heart.

Give a brief summary of what you've learned about your personal situation regarding your relationship with your mother, daughter or both.

_____

_____

_____

_____

_____

_____

Briefly write you're your plan is to do your part in mending or improving the relationship(s).

_____

_____

_____

_____

_____

_____

_____

Mom, Don't Get So Caught Up!
Mom, See Your Daughter

"They learned that if they called me "Mom" at church, I would seldom hear them; so they would call, "Sister Jeanie" and I would respond immediately..."   ***"Let the Healing Begin!" page 62, par.***

"...I was so caught up in my own world; from running with my "girlfriends", to running to church; taking a part-time job now and then, building relationship with my husband, then struggling in the relationship, serving at church, trying to please everyone outside the home, and trying to keep up my "religious self-image"...I was neglecting my children!..."   ***"Let the Healing Begin!" page 62, par. 2***

"When, where and why was Katrina spending that kind of time alone with him? And if this can happen while adults are in the home, what can happen when your children are home alone – kids babysitting kids? Think about it."   ***"Let the Healing Begin!" page 66, par.***

The previous chapters focused on MOM; her unresolved issues, what happened to her, what made her who she is. This chapter, Mom, is for you to focus on your daughter – regardless of her age or yours; age is not a factor. Regardless of your daughter's age, if you are going to mend or build a relationship with her, you are going to need to make it a priority. You relationship cannot and will not thrive on your leftover time.

The amount of time may vary however you want to make sure you are spending quality time. It's so easy to get "caught up", especially if you are a single mom working or going to school and/or have other children to tend to. If you are in ministry, volunteering, working or have any other major obligations – even just being a good friend or sibling; these can easily take priority over quality nurturing if you don't prioritize and be very purposeful in your planning.

In this lesson, you are going to begin a simple plan to include quality time for your relationship with your daughter. If your daughter is grown, obviously you will have to agree on the plan, so you want to keep it simple and flexible.

Once your list is prepared, call her, nail down some dates, and keep them!
Try to make it at least weekly, limiting texting.

FACE time = quality time!   HUG time = Healing time!

Suggestions:

- Movie night
- "Spa Day"
- Make a Scrapbook
- Gym
- Breakfast
- Lunch
- Dinner(eat out)
- Dinner (cook together)

My plan for quality time with my daughter is....

_____

_____

_____

_____

_____

_____

_____

_____

_____

_____

_____

This chapter is the cry of the inner thoughts, fears and emotions that paralyz or cripple so many people. This is a day and time when fear and insecurit  are prevalent like never before. Too often we depend on others to validate us, to make us feel secure – t make us feel that we are okay, that we matter. Man times, though, the very ones we are looking to ar depending on someone else for the same validation.

We are so concerned about what other people think o us that we wear masks; we are so afraid that if peopl see the real "us", they would reject us – Where does that come from? Who told us that we are less likeable than those to whom we look for affirmation?

We need people – positive people in our lives; relationships are important however, it doesn't matter how much you are appreciated, validated and esteemed by others, you will never rise to be your awesome, amazing and authentic self until you learn that YOUR VOICE is the loudest, the stronges and the most powerful voice you will ever hear. YOUR VOICE is the voice tha will dictate, that will dominate, and ultimately the only voice that wil motivate you to keep moving *(or get moving)* in the right direction, or to keep you on a downhill spiral. The initial negative thought or incident may have come from another source but your take-away becomes the voice in you head that perpetuates the negativity; it becomes your "self-talk".

What are you saying to yourself? Are you agreeing with the negative inne thoughts; the fears, the intimidating thoughts – are you a victim of the inne BULLYING that takes place when we don't stand up and resist those thoughts?

No matter how many times in a day someone else tells you that you have value, you have purpose, you are beautiful inside and out, etc. – if you don't believe it for yourself and let it truly become **your** inner voice; the most you will receive is a good feeling for the moment.

In this lesson, you are going to learn to find that inner voice and speak to yourself; to your insecurities, your fears – your feelings of inadequacy; those things that cripple you as an individual and become an adversary to any relationship. You are going to become empowered by YOUR own voice. You are not just reciting scripture or positive confessions; you are receiving, believing and accepting these truths for yourself, making them personal, making them your own. You are finding your OWN voice!

SELF TALK...

Make a list of 4 things **you can say to yourself** to resist the negative thoughts that come to taunt and bully you; these can be scriptures, quotes, or your own statements. Then write how you can do better in your relationship as a result. Keep them short but powerful; you will be more apt to memorize and use them.

*Ex: **God has good thoughts toward me every day. (Psalm 139)***
Result: I will think good thoughts toward my mother/daughter every day.

1. _____

    Result:_____

2. _____

    Result:_____

3. _____

    Result:_____

4. _____

    Result:_____

Self-Esteem: A Most Important Gift

"If you yield to another individual the right to assign your value, you are also yielding to them the right to take it away."

"Let the Healing Begin!" page 92, top of pag

Have you given up your rights? Yielded away your self-esteem? Dependin, on another or others to give you your value? Where does that leave you where does it leave your daughter? And her daughter(s)...and her daughters daughters?

This chapter has probably the most potential to change you and you daughter's lives. Please don't rush through it; in fact, I would suggest you g. through it a few times before you move on. The reason being that it needs t. become a part of you. This isn't just about actions – this is about changing . mind-set that you've probably had most of your life, and then going back fo your daughter; this is absolutely generational!

In previous chapters you went back to recover your voice and take your stor. back. This time we're going back specifically to see when and where your self esteem was damaged. Was it "taken" from you, as in a sexual assault, verba or physical abuse, etc., by bullying or mean kids at school making fun of you. Or did you give it up, allowing someone in your life who didn't care as mucl about you as you did about them and looking to them to validate you? Onc. you see where and how you lost it, you can use your inner voice to retrieve it You were not born with low self-esteem; this is what the Bible says abou how wonderfully God created you...

[1]O LORD, you have examined me, and You know me. [2]You alone knov when I sit down and when I get up. You read my thoughts from fa away... [13]You alone created my inner being. You knitted me togethe inside my mother. [14]I will give thanks to you because I have been sc amazingly and miraculously made..... [17]How precious are your thoughts concerning me, O God! PSALM 139:1-2, 13-14, 17

WHO, or WHAT spoke to you? Low self-esteem doesn't come simply because we get up one day and feel badly about ourselves. Someone or something speaks to you, you listen, and then your **self-talk** begins to agree with that negative "something" that lied to you about yourself. What was that "something"? How could it have had a different outcome? Who was saying what to you; and more importantly, what were you saying to yourself? Were you openly shamed – embarrassed, or "fronted", as we used to call it? Did you have an accident on yourself in school and the kids, just being kids, were amused without realizing how much it hurt when they laughed? Did you have a solo in church or school and choked? Were you molested, or raped? Let's examine – let's see what we can UN-do....

TAKE BACK YOUR SELF-ESTEEM!
(the one God created you with)

This exercise is similar to the previous one, except that we are specifically dealing with the self-esteem issue. Revisit the times you felt your self-esteem was damaged OR lifted. Where it was damaged, we want to change your story and take it back; where it was lifted, we want to retrieve it! Remember to do this in a quiet, secluded place and at a time when you won't be interrupted. Do this for as many incidents as you can remember *(not all at once, but not too far apart)*.

1. **ATMOSPHERE:** Close your eyes. Try to remember everything you can about the incident – do everything you can to put yourself back in that place...remember the atmosphere; was it dark, light – what time of day or night was it? What did the place smell like? Was it wet, dry – hot, cold... try to remember everything. Write it down.

2. **WHO:** Keeping your eyes closed...
   Who was there? *(write it down)* Who SHOULD have been there? Who should NOT have been there? Who do you WISH was there?

3. **WHAT:** What happened? *(just facts, not how you FELT – that comes later).* Was it physical, verbal? Was it something you SAW or HEARD? Was it good or bad? What did they say to you? What were you saying to YOURSELF?

4. **HOW:** How did it make you feel? Was your self-esteem damaged or lifted?

5. **USE YOUR VOICE:** If you could have said **anything** to **anybody,** what would you have said, and to whom? Write it down, as if you are there – say it to them.

6. **USE YOUR SELF-TALK:** From that incident, write down how your story changes – what are you saying to yourself now? What will you continue to say about yourself? It's not about the incident, it's about YOU – what are you saying about YOU?

7. **RETRIEVE IT:** If this was an incident that RAISED your self-esteem, bask in the moment; stay right there – what is being said to you? What are you saying to yourself? Write it down, repeat it until you believe it and retrieve it!

NOW take a moment to be quiet and let your inner self begin to heal. Don' *hold back any emotions or tears – that's why you are secluded...open up, let i* *out. Allow your tears to water the hardened ground of your heart and wash* *away the residue. Believe in the new you that emerges – it's the REAL YOU!*

CHAPTER 15

Discipline or Abuse?

What Is Child Abuse?

These important public health problems include all types of abuse and neglect of a child under the age of 18 by a parent, caregiver, or another person in a custodial role (such as clergy, a coach, a teacher) that results in harm, potential for harm, or threat of harm to a child. There are four common types of abuse and neglect, collectively referred to as child maltreatment:

- **Physical abuse** is the intentional use of physical force that can result in physical harm. Examples include hitting, kicking, shaking, burning, or other shows of force against a child.
- **Sexual abuse** involves pressuring or forcing a child to engage in sexual acts. It includes behaviors such as fondling, penetration, and exposing a child to other sexual activity.
- **Emotional abuse** refers to behaviors that harm a child's self-worth or emotional well-being. Examples include name calling, shaming, rejection, withholding love, and affection.
- **Neglect** is the failure to meet a child's basic physical and emotional needs. These needs include housing, food, clothing, education, and access to medical attention.

CDC (Centers for Disease Control and Prevention) Violence Prevention / Child Abuse and Neglect

What Causes Child Abuse to be transferred to the next generation?

Individual Risk Factors

- Parents' lack of understanding of children's needs, child development and parenting skills
- Parental history of child abuse and or neglect
- Substance abuse and/or mental health issues including depression in the family
- Parental characteristics such as young age, low education, single parenthood, large number of dependent children, and low income
- Nonbiological, transient caregivers in the home (e.g., mother's male partner)
- Parental thoughts and emotions that tend to support or justify maltreatment behaviors

CDC (Centers for Disease Control and Prevention) Violence Prevention / Child Abuse and Neglect

As we can see, there are many factors that may contribute to the forwarding of Child Abuse throughout the generations. We learn how to discipline from those who disciplined us – either what to do or what not to do. Many times what we learn **not** to do inadvertently becomes what we **do**. Consider this definition:

Punish: *1a : to impose a penalty on for a fault, offense, or violation*
b : to inflict a penalty for the commission of (an offense) in retribution or retaliation
2a : to deal with roughly or harshly
b : to inflict injury on : HURT   *Miriam Webster Dictionary*

There is sometimes a very thin line between *punishment* and *abuse*. One difference is the motive; are you trying to "inflict injury or pain" on your daughter because you are angry, frustrated or coming from the mindset that "you did wrong so you must "pay a penalty" – with no intention of teaching, training – no regard for her emotional well-being ? Or is your purpose truly a disciplinary action – for the purpose of teaching and training her to do better and make better choices? Sometimes abuse is applied simply because the parent, or adult authority, does not know any better. They do what they learned.

I am certainly not opposed to an occasional spanking – however, the very same action can be detrimental if not applied correctly; that is, with LOVE and understanding, and in the right place *(which is NEVER in the face).*

When your daughter is "punished" without understanding her error, all she can possibly receive from that is pain and confusion. *When she is punished outside of the margin of love*, and/or punished excessively, it may produce a measure of compliance, but can also cause her to become bitter, "hard" and eventually abusive to her own children.

An act of discipline is much more effective when she knows it comes from a place of love. In fact, many times when a child is disciplined in love, they don't have to revisit that same situation as often; because they know they are loved, they response is that they don't want to disappoint you. There are some "disciplinary actions" however, that should never be implemented, even with explanation and a heart of love.

Children need discipline, and sometimes that may even mean a spank on the butt – but NEVER in the face, NEVER with a cord of any type, NEVER with a fist.... these things only inflict pain, cause and contribute to low self-worth, and only serve to gratify the anger and frustration of the one inflicting the pain. **IT IS NEVER OKAY TO PUT WHELPS AND MARKS ON YOUR CHILD FROM "SPANKING" – THAT IS EXCESSIVE; IT IS CHILD ABUSE.**

Whether it is verbal or physical, whether it is a "grounding", a taking away of privileges, etc., the objective should be training, teaching and correction – to help the child become better and make better choices. Children should not be shamed or embarrassed in front of others – this, also, contributes to a low sense of self-worth or self-esteem.

This may be hard to accept, but some people do and have committed child abuse thinking they are doing the right thing, due to lack of knowledge, and they sincerely love their child. I know; I was one of them. But that does not make it any less abuse; it is no less painful, no less harm. That is the purpose for this chapter of the book and this exercise in the workbook – to show you a better way!

In disciplining, training, and/or correcting your daughter, you want her to always know that you are coming from a place of LOVE. You can accomplish this by:

- Showing her love on a daily basis.

- Talking to her about the issue; making clear boundaries <u>before</u> it becomes a problem.

- Giving her opportunity to show repentance; if she does on her own lessen the penalty. This teaches her mercy; to give it and receive it.

- Telling her that you love her and don't enjoy doing this and explainin why it is for her good.

- Letting her know how long the disciplinary action will last – let her se an end to it.

- Showing her GRACE in the midst of it *(she is grounded from TV for week? Order her favorite pizza and tell her you love her. Buy her a car that says, "I love you".)* This saturates the discipline with love.

- Talking to her; making sure she knows what her options are the nex time she faces this situation, and what her choice should be.

- Making it very clear to her what the consequences will be *(long and shor term)* for this type of action...

For example; (short term) For not completing your homework, you will lose TV and interne privileges until you are caught up. (long term) This will affect your learning sinc homework is designed to reinforce what you've learned. Ultimately it will affect you grades and possibly your future.... (Not that we want to lecture, but to help her to see th importance of those unwanted tasks.)

In disciplining, training, and/or correcting my daughter, I want her t always know that I am coming from a place of LOVE. I am going to work o that area by: *(List 45 things you will put in action to accomplish this goal)*

1. _____

   _____

2. _____

   _____

3. _____

   _____

4. _____

   _____

4 methods I will use to discipline, train and/or correct my daughter:

1. _____
   _____

2. _____
   _____

3. _____
   _____

4. _____
   _____

4 methods I will NEVER use to discipline, train and/or correct my daughter:

1. _____
   _____

2. _____
   _____

3. _____
   _____

4. _____
   _____

If you are or have been abusive to your daughter in any way, I pray your eyes have been opened – <u>without condemnation</u>, but with the determination to change. If you have been a victim of child abuse, I am so very sorry that you went through that and I hope you have found help and healing in these pages. I believe you are strong enough to decide that you will not forward this evil to the next generation. There is no shame in asking for help; the shame is in continuing to hurt an innocent child.

Did you know that child abuse is an offense against your child, a sin against God and a very serious criminal act?

If you have had any issues with child abuse, whether as the victim or th abuser, please consider seriously and aggressively acting immediately t correct this issue, protecting your daughter as well as yourself.

This is a pledge we can all commit to....

My home is a NO CHILD ABUSE HOME!

I pledge never to commit, condone or keep silent about child abuse of any typ in my home, my family or my community. participate in child abuse of an type.

I will allow my family and friends to keep me accountable to this pledge. I giv my daughter and any other children in my home permission to answer an questions from those who are holding me accountable. I also am willing t answer questions from those who hold me accountable.

I understand that family and friends hold each other accountable because w love each other and our children, who deserve to be loved, happy and SAFE ir their environment. Therefore, I will educate myself as well as being teachable making certain that I know the difference between chastisement, disciplin and abuse. I will educate my child(ren) about child abuse and will not allow this to be a part of our family legacy. I will teach my child(ren) to speak up fo themselves and speak out about child abuse, in or out of the home.

I am signing this commitment because I love my child(ren) and as a mother, i is my responsibility to see that they live in a safe and loving environment.

Sincerely _____   Date _____

CHAPTER 16
Where Do We Go From Here?"

Well - It looks like we've come to the end of this workbook, which, FOR YOU, is only the beginning – a NEW beginning for your mother-daughter relationship, which means a new hope and a new future; a new chance for a healthy family tree! I am so glad, so honored and so proud of you for working through this book! I'm so happy for you and your new mother-daughter relationship and excited for what lies ahead!

So, where do you go from here? You go on to a better, much happier and more fulfilling relationship! You go down in your family history as one who eradicated the dysfunction in the family tree! You are a "She-ro"!

You have learned some new methods and you have walked through some painful "stronghold-shattering" exercises - all for the sake of becoming that mother, that daughter, who is a cheerleader, best friend, confidant, encourager and life-til-death support for the mother/daughter God hand-picked just for you.

KEEP READING TO THE END*; In the next few pages I've included some guidelines to continue the process after the healing begins....how to keep the ground you've covered; to maintain your new relationship, even when the old tries to rear its ugly head. COMMUNICATION IS KEY!*

Please keep this book in a safe place *– revisit it from time to time; you'd be amazed the things you see when you go back and look again. I've prayed with you through this journey and will continue to pray with you. You have the website, Facebook, email – please keep in touch and know that there is a whole team of people holding you and your mother/daughter(s) up in prayer. God is with you; you can love – unconditionally. Let the HEALING begin!*

Guidelines for the PROCESS

1. If you are unable to keep your agreed time with her, let her know that you ar committed to this process, and tell her when you will get together – say it like yo really mean it, and follow through.

2. Tread carefully – deal with one issue at a time.

3. Don't let every conversation be about solving issues; work on enjoying eac other's company.

4. Always keep her confidence. Just because your friends are your friends, tha does not give you the right to discuss her business. A sure way to build anothe wall – besides, a real integrity issue!

5. Even if you've had a difficult or unpleasant conversation, try to end on a goo note. She won't want to talk again if she feels bad afterward. Try to end with a hug, even if it feels awkward.

6. Try to see the situation from her side; put yourself in her place and consider she may have a valid point of view.

7. With each issue, look for a pattern – how did your mom deal with this? How did HER mom deal with it? Then examine and decide whether this is a practice that should be continued or discontinued; you can learn from their mistakes.

It's not always the right time to have an in-depth conversation, just as it's no always the right time to do a thorough cleaning of your house. Sometimes it's more expedient to "sweep the dirt under the rug" for the moment. Bu then, make sure you return soon to sweep under the rug. If you keep sweeping the dirt under the rug and never return to sweep under the rug eventually somebody's going to trip and fall! You must revisit the conversation and get closure, understanding and forgiveness, so you can **Let the Healing Begin!**

Guidelines for COMMUNICATION

❖ Focus on solving a problem; reaching a solution rather than venting your anger or winning a victory; this means, agreeing to disagree on some points.

❖ Deal with one issue at a time. It's neither fair nor productive to pile several complaints into one session.

❖ Attack the issue, not the person. Name-calling and verbally attacks put her in a position to respond angrily and defensively. This breaks down communication and destroys trust.

❖ If necessary, take a time-out. Take a short break to cool off, calm down and get perspective.

❖ "You Always"… "You Never." are usually exaggerations and will put the other person on the defensive.

❖ Listen to HEAR, not to REPLY. Try – really try, to put yourself in her place to hear what she is saying. Listen beyond her words; Try to hear her heart.

❖ Be respectful; using put-down words or statements such as dumb, stupid, lazy, etc. will only escalate animosity and certainly build a wall.

❖ Avoid interrupting, talking over or make comments while the other is speaking. Negative body language; rolling eyes, smirking, yawning, etc. are all counter-productive, and not respectful.

❖ Be quick to apologize, and quick to accept an apology; even if you feel it is not sincere. Choose to believe it is sincere, forgive, and move forward.

❖ Try to use your words and character and explain your heart rather than to try to force or threaten; that is counter-productive.

❖ If you need to leave or hang up the phone, tell her you need to take a break and will be back (or call back) when you've calmed down.

❖ Be merciful; if you see that your words are hurting her – even if they are true, be gentle, tread lightly. She may need a break; be open to that.

COMPLETE THESE SENTENCES

1. I love myself because...

   _____
   _____
   _____

2. One thing I do really well is....

   _____
   _____

3. My friends say I am the best at...

   _____
   _____

4. My favorite place is...

   _____

5. People say I'm a good...

   _____

6. I feel good about myself when I....

   _____
   _____

7. I consider myself to be a good...

   _____

8. I am loved by...

   _____
   _____
   _____

Thank you so much for walking out your confession of love for your mother, your daughter(s). I trust this has been a life-changing, family-changing, and generation-changing experience. I pray you will pass it on; that you will share your experience, share the book, **"Let the Healing Begin"** (don't give up YOURS; share the information!), and above all, I have every confidence that you found the tools you need to allow healing to begin in your relationships, and that you are inspired to be a nurturer to the "motherless daughters" that God sends along your pathway. Let the Healing Begin!!

God bless you - Love you much!!
Jeanie Robinson

Facebook:
Let the Healing Begin
Imogene Brown-Robinson @ healing begins 2019

Email: HealingBegins2019@gmail.com

55230388R00037

Made in the USA
Columbia, SC
11 April 2019